D0358492

The Amazon

Jane Bingham

www.raintreepublishers.co.uk
Visit our website to find out
more information about
Raintree books.

To order:
☎ Phone 0845 6044371
🖸 Fax +44 (0) 1865 312263
🖂 Email myorders@raintreepublishers.co.uk

Customers from outside the UK please telephone +44 1865 312262

Raintree is an imprint of Capstone Global Library
Limited, a company incorporated in England and
Wales having its registered office at 7 Pilgrim Street,
London, EC4V 6LB – Registered company number:
6695582

Edited by Rebecca Rissman, Dan Nunn, and
    Catherine Veitch
Designed by Cynthia Della-Rovere
Levelling by Jeanne Clidas
Picture research by Elizabeth Alexander
Production by Victoria Fitzgerald
Originated by Capstone Global Library
Printed and bound in China by CTPS

ISBN 978 1 406 24188 4
16 15 14 13 12
10 9 8 7 6 5 4 3 2 1

British Library Cataloguing in Publication Data
Bingham, Jane.
The Amazon. -- (Explorer tales)
918.1'1'04-dc22
A full catalogue record for this book is available from
the British Library.

Acknowledgements
We would like to thank the following for permission
to reproduce photographs: Alamy pp. 6 (© Susan E.
Degginger), 8 (© North Wind Picture Archives), 9 (©
The Art Gallery Collection), 10 (© David Tomlinson),
12 (© Travel Elite Images), 16 (© Pictorial Press Ltd),
21 (© The Art Archive), 27 (© SnapperUK), 28 (© The
Print Collector), 29 (© INTERFOTO); Corbis p. 11 (©
Bettmann); Dreamstime.com p. 5 (© Jlye); FLPA pp. 18
(© James Christensen/Minden Pictures), 19 (© Michael
& Patricia Fogden/Minden Pictures); Getty Images
pp. 7 (luoman/Vetta), 22 (Universal History Archive/
Hulton Archive), 26 (Fernanda Preto/LatinContent),
public domain p. 24; Shutterstock pp. 14 (© JaySi), 20
(© Dr. Morley Read), 25 (© costas anton dumitrescu);
TopFoto p. 15 (The Granger Collection).

Cover photographs of Alexander von Humboldt
reproduced with permission of Corbis (© Bettmann);
section of South America, 1806, Terra Firma, Peru,
Brazil reproduced with permission of Sanders of
Oxford, rare prints & maps (www.sandersofoxford.
com); wooden bungalows, Amazon River, Brazil
reproduced with permission of Shutterstock (©
JaySi). Interior background photograph of wooden
bungalows, Amazon River, Brazil reproduced with
permission of Shutterstock (© JaySi).

Every effort has been made to contact copyright
holders of material reproduced in this book. Any
omissions will be rectified in subsequent printings if
notice is given to the publisher.

Contents

Some words are shown in bold, **like this**. You can find out what they mean by looking in the glossary.

The Amazon rainforest is steamy, dark, and dangerous. It is home to millions of creatures and plants. In the heart of the forest is the Amazon River. It runs for over 6,000 kilometres across South America.

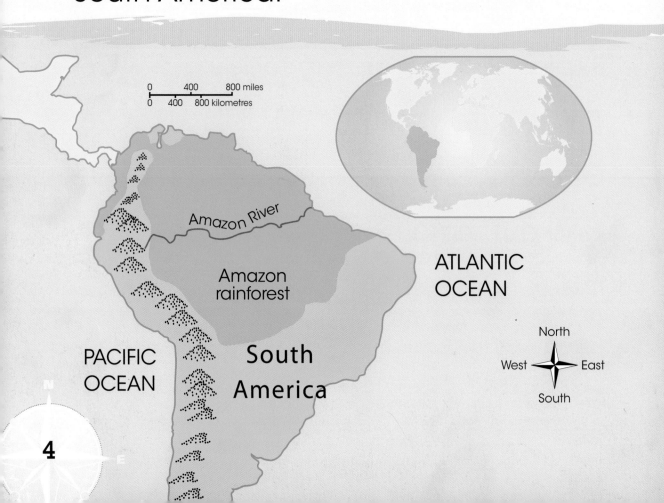

0   400   800 miles
0   400   800 kilometres

Amazon River

Amazon
rainforest

ATLANTIC
OCEAN

PACIFIC
OCEAN

South
America

North

West — East

South

DID YOU KNOW?
The Amazon rainforest is so huge it would cover two-thirds of the United States.

jaguar

The rainforest is full of hidden dangers. Jaguars wait silently, ready to pounce. Snakes glide through the trees. Deadly piranha fish swim in the rivers. Piranha fish can strip the flesh from your bones in just five minutes!

The native Amazon people know how to survive in the forest. They are expert hunters and farmers.

Searching for gold

In the 1500s, some brave explorers left Europe. They headed for South America. The explorers had heard stories about a city of gold. The stories said **El Dorado** was ruled by a magical, golden king.

Francisco de Orellana was a Spanish explorer. In 1541, he led an **expedition** to search for **El Dorado**. After 10 months, the explorers ran out of food. But Orellana had a plan. He ordered his men to build a boat. Then he set off with 50 men. He promised he would return with food.

Spanish explorers met the local people.

Orellana's boat was carried very fast down the Napo River (see the map on page 13). In August 1542, the explorers reached the Amazon River.

River travel can be very dangerous!

ATLANTIC OCEAN

0   400   800 miles

0   400   800 kilometres

Orellana's route

Quito

Napo River

Amazon River

PACIFIC OCEAN

mountains

North

West — East

South

13

Most Amazon homes are built on stilts because the river often floods.

The explorers rowed slowly down the Amazon River. They saw many villages and farms. Some **native** people gave them food. Some shot poison arrows at their boat! Finally, the explorers reached the Atlantic Ocean. They were the first European people to travel all the way down the Amazon River.

Orellana and his men would have travelled in a boat like this.

In 1749, a man called Jean Godin travelled from Riobamba to Cayenne (see the map on page 17). This was a journey of more than 5,000 kilometres. Jean left his wife, Isabela, behind in Riobamba.

Isabela and Jean lived apart for many years.

Jean thought he would soon return home. But he was not allowed to leave Cayenne. After many years of living alone, Jean sent a boat to Lagunas to wait for Isabela.

Riobamba

Cayenne

ATLANTIC OCEAN

Amazon River

Lagunas

PACIFIC OCEAN

Isabela's route

0   400   800 miles
0   400   800 kilometres

North
West — East
South

Before she could catch the boat, Isabela had to reach Lagunas. In 1769, she set off with 42 people. They crossed the Andes Mountains and **trekked** through the forest. Some of the travellers died from **exhaustion**. Some were attacked by vampire bats. Only Isabela was left alive.

DID YOU KNOW?
Vampire bats can carry a deadly disease called **rabies**.

Isabela **staggered** on through the rainforest. After nine days, she met some **native** people. They took care of her until she was stronger. Then they took her to her boat.

The boat took Isabela all the way down the Amazon River. Then it travelled up the coast to Cayenne. At last Isabela and Jean were together again!

Isabela would have travelled on a boat like this.

The man who loved birds

Henry Bates was a wildlife expert. In 1848, he went to South America to search for rare creatures. At first he lived in Pará, close to the sea. But he wanted to travel deep into the rainforest. So he set off down the Amazon River.

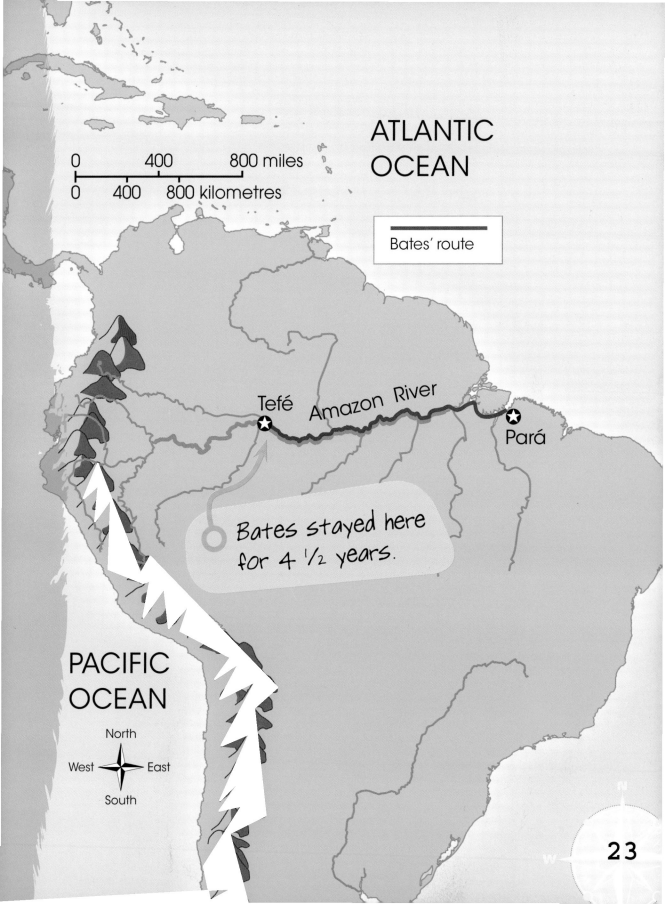

ATLANTIC OCEAN

0   400   800 miles
0   400   800 kilometres

—— Bates' route

Tefé   Amazon River   Pará

Bates stayed here for 4 ½ years.

PACIFIC OCEAN

North
West —✦— East
South

Bates stayed in the rainforest for 11 years in total. He saw **toucans** with huge, colourful bills. He saw tiny **hummingbirds** and giant spiders. He even saw a spider eating a bird!

DID YOU KNOW?

Bates nursed a sick toucan back to health. The bird became his friend, and they shared all their meals.

Exploring the Amazon today

People still explore the Amazon today. Explorers search for lost cities. Scientists look for plants. In the 21st century, the Amazon is still a place of mystery and excitement.

Scientists dig for pottery that belonged to people long ago.

DID YOU KNOW?

Plants from the Amazon rainforest are used in medicines for treating many illnesses today.

1500s	Explorers from Spain and Portugal start to travel in South America.
1541– 1542	Francisco Orellana and his crew travel the whole length of the Amazon River.
1769– 1770	Isabela Godin travels from Riobamba to Cayenne.
1848– 1859	Henry Bates explores the Amazon rainforest.

El Dorado magical city rich in gold

exhaustion condition where a person does not have much strength and is too tired to carry on

expedition long journey to explore a place

hummingbird tiny bird that is the same size as a butterfly

native person born in a particular place. Native Amazon people were born in the Amazon.

rabies very serious disease that usually kills people

stagger walk in a very unsteady way

toucan bird with a large, brightly-coloured beak

trek walk a very long way, often across rough ground

Books

Living in the Amazon Rainforest (World Cultures),
    Anita Ganeri, (Raintree, 2008)

Rainforests (Espresso Ideas Box!),
    Deborah Chancellor, (Franklin Watts, 2011)

The Vanishing Rainforest, Richard Platt
    (Frances Lincoln, 2007)

Websites

**www.nationalgeographic.com/features/00/
earthpulse/rainforest/index_flash-feature.html**
Explore the sights and sounds of the rainforest
at night.

www.pbs.org/journeyintoamazonia/
Play the game "Amazon explorer" and discover
the forest's secrets.

Index